WELCOME T
HOLISTICALLY Fi
WELLNESS MINDSET JOURNAL

Hello and welcome to your very own Wellness Mindset Journal. Congratulations on making the choice to get to know yourself better. This journal helps you gain a better Connection with yourself gives you more Clarity and Control of your life. and ultimately boosts up your Confidence.

Mindfulness is all about having a Conscious Connection (or in simpler terms - awareness) with yourself - of your thoughts, your feelings and your actions.

Being Mindful allows you to connect your Mind, Body and Soul as one to enable you to create a more positive life with more meaning, fun and happiness. It's a Holistic approach to living.

This journal allows you the opportunity to kickstart your mindful journey of yourself and your life - to shift your mindset and lift into more conscious awareness / connection so that you can step away from the stress and chaos surrounding you and step into a life with more energy, peace and meaning.

Of course it's really important to work on the "external" part of your life - such as keeping your body fit, eating balanced and nutritious whole foods and taking time out to breathe and connect - however getting your mind right is the key to sustainable healthy living and maintaining a balanced and healthy lifestyle.

This is your life and your journey - and everything you do, think & feel all comes down to the CHOICES you make.
This journal will help you kickstart your connection to yourself!

MINDSET *Journal*

XO
Sally

H F HOLISTICALLYFIT
EMPOWER YOURSELF INSIDE + OUT

GLOBAL WELLNESS ECONOMY:
$4.2 trillion in 2017

Traditional & Complementary Medicine
$360b

Wellness Real Estate
$134b

Wellness Tourism
$639b

Personal Care, Beauty & Anti-Aging
$1,083b

Preventive & Personalized Medicine and Public Health
$575b

Workplace Wellness
$48b

Thermal/Mineral Springs
$56b

Healthy Eating, Nutrition & Weight Loss
$702b

Fitness & Mind-Body
$595b

Spa Economy
$119b

The world is starting to wake up and become more in touch. According to the Global Wellness Institute the rapidly growing wellness market is worth $4.2 trillion USD. From 2015-2017, the wellness economy grew 6.4% annually, nearly twice as fast as global economic growth (3.6%).

The World Health Organisation (WHO) recently recognised Burn Out as an occupational syndrome from "chronic workplace stress that has not been successfully managed" - "characterised by 3 dimensions 1) feelings of energy depletion or exhaustion; 2) increased mental distance from one's job, or feelings of negativism or cynicism related to one's job; and 3) reduced professional efficacy."

Isn't it time to give yourself a makeover? Get some energy back, reduce your stress and live a simpler life?

Imagine you have a big cup full of water and that represents your time, energy and life right now. What if you could tip out some of the things in your life that aren't serving you and fill up with more soul satisfying activities. How awesome would you feel!

Use this journal as a guide to get you focused on yourself and shifting your life so you can lift into being more mindful of yourself and your choices.

MINDSET
Journal

HOLISTICALLYFIT

GLOBAL WELLNESS INSTITUTE

HOW TO
GET THE MOST OUT OF YOUR JOURNAL

This is a 30 day journal designed for you to check in, assess and set some actions for the day as well as reflect upon yourself and the choices you have made.

To really get the most out of your journal let's recap on what all these areas of mindfulness really mean. Don't worry if it all seems a bit too much at the start. Just start and take small steps. As you progress throughout the journal - you will find it easier to complete and to assess yourself.

Doing the "inner" work can be challenging and confronting - but that's OK - be gentle on yourself. Congratulate yourself for embarking on this journey and becoming more consciously connected with yourself. What would your life be like if you didn't?

Here are some descriptions of areas that are covered and this glossary will help you understand how to complete your journal.

GLOSSARY

MANIFESTING - Your daily manifestation exercise

Manifesting is a very powerful tool where you choose to bring positive things into your life which ultimately enhance your quality of living.

Manifesting is more than just choosing something nice to come into your life - it's about really marrying the positive feelings you can visualise with those choices / intentions and then having the gratitude for them happening - feeling grateful in the present time - as if you have it already.

Don't worry if you have never done any manifesting before.

As with everything - just start with simple, small steps. The more you do them - the easier it becomes.

GLOSSARY

Simple Steps to Manifesting:

- **CHOOSE** the things you would like to manifest into your life.
- **TRUST and BELIEVE** in yourself that you are worthy and it IS possible and can happen.
- **VISUALISE** the things you are choosing.
- **FEEL** the emotions of having those things - how you feel as if you have them right now in the present time - as if it has already happened = see it, feel it, hear it, sense it.
- **GRATITUDE** - Really feel the gratitude for having those things - imagine you already have them and how grateful you feel for it.
- **RELEASE and LET GO** - Don't think about HOW it's going to happen or WHEN - just allow and trust that the Universe is taking care of it. Once you've chosen your manifestations - release and let go so you can receive. Make space for the new choices to come in.

The key to successful manifestations: The greater you match your EMOTIONS (how awesome you feel as if you already have it) with your MANIFESTATIONS and the GRATITUDE = the stronger the "signal" you are sending out. TRUST and BELIEVE it will happen and then LET IT GO. Don't overthink it. The Universe works in magical ways - and these manifestations often occur when you least expect them.

An example of manifesting: I choose to increase my savings by $10,000 within 3 months easily and effortlessly. I am so grateful for cash flowing into my savings account - it fills me with such joy and happiness.

 MEDITATION

Meditation is a powerful way of connecting inwardly and turning off from the outside world. It allows you to tune into yourself and go to a place of calm and peace away from the stress and chaos around you. Meditation comes in many forms - you can do it walking, lying down, sitting etc and in all sorts of situations such as yoga.

Meditation in the morning is a perfect way to kickstart your day and set your intentions for the day ahead. It is also an awesome time to manifest things you are choosing to bring into your life.

GLOSSARY

A simple way to meditate is to tune into your breath. Focusing on breathing in through your nose and out through your mouth. It's about connecting and focusing inwardly. Meditation is best done in a quiet space and allows you to connect in on a deeper level.
If you haven't meditated before or find it challenging - just start with simple, small steps. Download an app that resonates with you. Like anything in life - the more you practice - the easier it will become.

AFFIRMATIONS

Affirmations are words you use to shift your energy from negative thought patterns and lift you to more positive, heightened emotions. Such as I am an awesome person, I can do anything I put my mind to, I am worthy of love, I choose to be the best version of myself, I choose to be consciously connected with myself, I have unlimited potential ...

GRATITUDE

Being grateful is one of the most vital ways to shift into positivity and lift everything into perspective. When we sit with gratitude - we can let things go and reduce the stress. The Universe LOVES it when we are grateful. We can be grateful for past experiences, present time events and grateful for what we are bringing into our lives - feeling as we if we already have it now.

PLAN, ACTION & REWARD

Planning and prioritising your tasks each day help shift you from the stress and overwhelm and lift you into actioning and completing simple, small tasks which you can tick off.
It's really important to reward yourself for getting stuff done. What have you achieved today and how are you rewarding yourself? By acknowledging your "wins" you keep inspired and motivated and feel a sense of achievement.

Plan - Prioritise your to do list and what needs to be done.
Prioritise activities which satisfy your soul not crush it.
Action - Implement the work.
Reward - Acknowledge completion of a task and give yourself a pat on the back - reward yourself!

GLOSSARY

POSITIVITY - POSITIVE BELIEFS

Limiting Beliefs -
Rewiring your SELF HEAD TALK: the Inner Critic vs the Inner Coach

A lot of our thoughts about ourselves and our attitude towards things have been created from a very young age. Most of us don't even realise that we run through our days with these old, out of date belief patterns - based on experiences that occurred way back when we were kids.

Have a think about some of the limiting beliefs you may be carrying with you subconsciously/unconsciously - do they need updating?

FOR EXAMPLE:

Do you think you're not good enough - you'll never be as good as that other person? You're not capable of achieving greatness? These type of limiting beliefs just hold you back. They aren't really true - just part of your old belief patterns. Let's update them! Once you have the awareness of the things you've been telling yourself - then you are able to change them.

We all have an inner voice that is our Inner Critic. That voice which is so quick to put you down and sabotage your best intentions. You can overcome this Inner Critic by boosting up your Inner Coach. The other side of you that says "For sure you can do it - you're awesome and you're more than capable". The more you silence that Inner Critic and allow the Inner Coach to shine - the quicker you can successfully sustain the changes you want to bring into your life and achieve the results you are aiming for.

So step into your Inner Coach and allow yourself to be the best version of yourself and tell that Inner Critic to bugger off.

In this journal everyday you are asked to fill out a positive belief you truly believe about yourself deep down inside. Renew your thoughts of yourself and build up that Inner Coach with positive, inspiring beliefs about yourself.

GLOSSARY

POSITIVITY EXCERCISE

There are always positives to be found in any perceived negative situation. When we take a more in depth look at the situation at hand you can shift your energy back into the positive by analysing what positives you can take out of it.

FOR EXAMPLE:

Having a cold. You might perceive it as a negative because you feel yuk and you can't function efficiently and just want to curl up in bed. However when you look at the positives it can shift your mindset around it - such as - this is only a temporary set back, you are usually healthy. By feeling poorly - it allows you to cut out a lot of the "daily" activities that you usually do - and encourages you to focus on only a few simple things you can get done. It's allowing your body to rest and strengthen. It also provides a time of reflection - have you been doing too much? Getting too run down? Have you been eating nutritious foods or getting enough sleep?

By lifting into the positive of any perceived negative situation - it allows you to put the situation into a better perspective. On the "catastrophe scale" is it really the worst thing that can be happening to you? Eg: death would be high on the catastrophe scale vs not getting your work in by the deadline. Is it life or death?

Each day - take one perceived negative situation and assess the positives you can take out of it. Shift your mindset.

DOWNTIME / CHILL

What have you done to chill out today - how much downtime have you had? It's so important to balance your time and energy with things that help you turn off and wind down. Give yourself some downtime. Even if it's taking an hour out at the end of the day and chilling out with a long bath, some soothing music or watching a bit of Netflix.

Take time out to wind down and chill out from the stresses and routine of your day. Do you prioritise enough "me time"?

SELF LOVE

Self love is about nurturing the love for yourself. Self love is often a challenging subject for many people. It requires you to look at yourself in a mirror and truly see the beauty of you within. The more you can tap into the authentic love you have for yourself - the higher you vibrate outwardly. Your confidence skyrockets, you find it a lot easier to "Let Stuff Go" - and you are more capable of implementing healthy boundaries in your life and can say NO more easily.

You'll find you stop trying to please everyone else so much and you just become way more comfortable in your own skin. Self love allows you to love yourself more honestly and enables you to have better quality relationships with others. It allows you to be more authentic in the way you act, feel and think.

ICONS

Mindfulness is not just about the health of your mind but also about your body functioning optimally as well. There's a daily check in to mark off the icons as reminders to keep regular structure and balance in all these areas.

EXERCISE

It's so important to exercise your body, mind and soul every day. What have you done today? Meditate, yoga, workout, walk, cardio or stretch /breathe? There are so many benefits to exercise - as well as maintaining a healthy body you are also helping prevent illness down the track Improve your posture, flexibility and strength, and get the body flowing freer. Make it a priority in your everyday schedule!

NUTRITION

You are what you eat! Your diet contributes to about 80% of your weight - but what you eat also has a dramatic impact on the way you feel and your overall health. Gut health is paramount for a healthy mindset - so what does your diet look like? If you suffer from brain fog, lack of concentration, sluggish digestion etc- the odds are that your diet needs reviewing. Less sugar and processed and refined foods is a very good start. Reduce inflammation in your gut. It's all about what you eat, when you eat, how much you eat and why you eat.

SLEEP

Your quality of sleep is super important for so many reasons - especially so you can wake up refreshed, rejuvenated and reinvigorated to start your day positive and ready to go. Do you have a regular bedtime - do you have a wind down process prior to bed? So many factors affect a good sleep - is your sleep environment adequate?

HYDRATION

It's so important to hydrate with water everyday - support the healthy eco system of your body - such as your brain, blood, organs and also remove toxins. It's important to consume 2+ litres/day. Did you know 80% of people are dehydrated? Do you drink enough water everyday?

TIME / ENERGY BALANCE

We all have limited time and energy per day. So many people push through their days, run out of time, have no time for themselves and end up exhausted. Are your days balanced?

Choose your time and energy wisely. Put some healthy boundaries in place and learn to say NO more often. It's not always easy - and it's often the most exhausted ones who do everything for everyone else and put themselves last. Is this you? Throughout your journal try and focus on bringing more balance into your days.

START WITH INTENTION

Write down and set your positive intentions here.
What are your mindful intentions for the next 30 days?
What do you hope to achieve, change or learn?

NAME _____ DATE _____ / _____ / _____

WHERE YOU ARE NOW SNAPSHOT - SELF ASSESSMENT

Before you begin your journal entries, complete your initial self assessment below by circling honestly where you are now in each of the fields. This will help you review your progress throughout your journey.

AFFIRMATIONS	NEVER	SOMETIMES	WEEKLY	DAILY				
MANIFESTING	NEVER	SOMETIMES	WEEKLY	DAILY				
GRATITUDE	NEVER	SOMETIMES	WEEKLY	DAILY				
MEDITATION	NEVER	SOMETIMES	WEEKLY	DAILY				
EXERCISE	NEVER	SOMETIMES	1X WEEK	2X WEEK	3X WEEK +			
NUTRITION	UNHEALTHY	0	1	2	3	4	5	HEALTHY/BALANCED
WATER INTAKE	NONE	0	1	2	3	4	5	2+ LITRES A DAY
SLEEP QUALITY	NOT RESTED	0	1	2	3	4	5	WELL RESTED
ME TIME	NONE AT ALL	0	1	2	3	4	5	EVERYDAY
SELF LOVE	LOW	0	1	2	3	4	5	HIGH
SELF TALK/HEAD TALK	NEGATIVE	0	1	2	3	4	5	POSITIVE
OVERALL FEELING	STUCK/DOWN	0	1	2	3	4	5	HAPPY/BALANCED
OVERALL HAPPINESS	NOT HAPPY	0	1	2	3	4	5	VERY HAPPY
OVERALL STRESS	LOW STRESS	0	1	2	3	4	5	HIGH STRESS
OVERALL ENERGY	LOW ENERGY	0	1	2	3	4	5	HIGH ENERGY
OVERALL FUN	NO FUN	0	1	2	3	4	5	LOADS OF FUN

SIMPLE, SMALL STEPS TO BE:
MORE MINDFUL, CONSCIOUS, CONNECTED & AWARE

- **Live** in the PRESENT time - it's the only headspace to be in.
- **Stop** worrying about tomorrow or getting stuck in the past.
- **Think** about the impact if you stay on the same path you are on now - how will it continue to affect you and what will happen down the track?
- **Be** accountable for the choices you make - own them and then don't stress about them. Just relax. What's done is done.
- **Reduce** your stress - relax and breathe - focus on your breath to help you connect back with yourself - reduce your stress and be more calm. Do more of the things that relax you.
- **Balance** your energy. Try and reduce doing things or hanging around people who wear you out or drain you emotionally.
- **Shift** your mindset to think positively. There are positives to be found with every single situation - it helps you shift perceived negative situations into the positive and give you better perspective.
- **Let** S*%t GO! Prioritise your days to focus on things that really matter and also on things that bring you Joy, Happiness and Fun! Create a simpler life.
- **Surround** yourself with like minded positive people - hang with a tribe who fill your heart with joy and give your soul satisfaction.
- **Be** selective where and with whom you choose to spend your time and energy - they are your precious commodities so choose wisely!
- **Remember** this is YOUR journey through life and make conscious choices that bring you Joy and Happiness.
- **Exercise** your Body, Mind and Soul. Be active daily - stretch, connect with your breath, tone and strengthen your body. Activate your mind in positive ways. Reconnect with your soul - your inner self. Love yourself more and be gentle and kind to yourself with your words, thoughts and actions.
  Get all your muscles moving - your brain, heart and body!
- **Eat well** - there is a 3-way connection between your brain, gut and heart. What you eat impacts directly with the way you feel and think. Eat healthy foods for a healthy mindset.
- **To be** Consciously Connected means you are AWARE of yourself and what's going on in your world. The better you truly know yourself - the more you can understand how you tick and why you make the choices you do!

SIMPLE, SMALL STEPS TO BE:
MORE MINDFUL, CONSCIOUS, CONNECTED & AWARE

- **Have** time out for yourself everyday to chill and just BE.
- **Hydrate** your body. Our bodies and brain, heart and lungs are predominantly composed of water - so keep up your daily water intake to keep clear, focused and operating efficiently!
- **Do** things that bring you JOY and FUN.
- **Think** happy thoughts about yourself. Silence the self sabotaging Inner Critic in your head and boost up the Inner Coach. You are AWESOME and become your own coach. Motivate, inspire and boost yourself up. You're the best person for the job!
- **Use** daily affirmations to shift and lift your energy to positive thoughts about yourself and the world around you.
- **Talk** yourself up. By verbally talking to yourself you are bringing your thoughts and energy out of your "inside" and bringing them into the present moment and into your conscious awareness. It's super powerful - try it!
- **Renew** the limiting beliefs you have about yourself.
  Think about the things you "believe" about yourself, assess them and say to yourself "hey - these aren't really true". Update them and step into truly believing that you are capable of doing anything you want.
- **Get** some good quality sleep - implement some healthy habits before bedtime such as dimming the lights, having some downtime, not eating too late and getting off your phone; have a good sleep environment (dark, cool room with weighted blankets) and where possible have a regular bedtime. Try having an epsom salt bath or a herbal tea.
- **Practice** being grateful - every day think about what you are truly grateful for - it shifts your mind into being more positive.
- **Meditate** often! It's a great practice to get you grounded, centred, connected and relaxed - plus it's a great platform to bring in your manifestations.
- **Smile** and laugh more. It makes you look younger, makes people feel more comfortable and is good for your soul!
- **Reward** your achievements - reward yourself often - as it inspires, motivates and acknowledges your achievements.
- **Be** your authentic self - align how you feel on the inside with how people perceive you. Let the world see the genuine you - you'll feel so much more relaxed just being yourself.
- **TRUST and BELIEVE** in you! That's the key to progress!

aware present
journey wellness
achieve lovable
goals self conciously success
love experience simple body
control balance guide
trust believe grateful
today reward
worthy
lance fitness practise happiness outcome
ydration change
love chakra clarity lifestyle
nifesting visualise energy
stunning self
feel resonate calm beliefs soul
yes fit
holistic life
abundance chilled say respect motivation mind
meditation thrive
create worth treat at restore
selfselfself life motivation
start smile quiet fun
confidence personal
ity time thrive allow
tion

HF HOLISTICALLY**FIT**
EMPOWER YOURSELF INSIDE + OUT

DAY 1

AM

DATE:

Fill in 3 daily affirmations to keep your energy positive and build yourself up & 3 things you are grateful for.
Finally write out your daily manifestation for what you choose to bring into your life, with gratitude and feeling
as if you already have it now (your manifestation may be the same as the day before but it's important to write it out).

AFFIRMATIONS	GRATITUDE	DAILY MANIFESTATION
# 1	# 1	
# 2	# 2	
# 3	# 3	

PLAN ~ ACTION ~ REWARD

PLAN   Write down the things you choose to ACHIEVE TODAY

ACTION   Write down THE TASKS to achieve your plan

REWARD   Write down how you will REWARD yourself for completing your plan

WRITE 1 POSITIVE BELIEF ABOUT YOURSELF BELOW:

QUOTE OF THE DAY
It's your time to shine!

POSITIVITY

Write down something negative you experienced today - then under it list the positives you can take out of that experience

SELF LOVE

What activities have you done to nurture your love for yourself?

DOWNTIME / CHILL

What did you do to chill out today or to wind down and give yourself a break?

HOW HAPPY DID YOU FEEL TODAY?

  0   1   2   3   4   6   7   8   9   10   😄

USE ONE WORD TO DESCRIBE HOW YOU ARE FEELING:

WHAT DID YOU DO THAT WAS FUN TODAY?

ENERGY

WHAT'S BEEN DRAINING YOUR
ENERGY TODAY?

WHAT'S BOOSTED YOUR
ENERGY TODAY?

STRESS

WHAT'S ADDED TO THE STRESS
IN YOUR DAY?

WHAT'S HELPED TO REDUCE
YOUR STRESS TODAY?

DAY 2

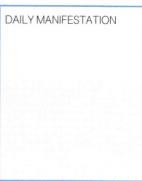

AM

DATE:

Fill in 3 daily affirmations to keep your energy positive and build yourself up & 3 things you are grateful for.
Finally write out your daily manifestation for what you choose to bring into your life, with gratitude and feeling
as if you already have it now (your manifestation may be the same as the day before but it's important to write it out).

AFFIRMATIONS	GRATITUDE	DAILY MANIFESTATION
# 1	# 1	
# 2	# 2	
# 3	# 3	

PLAN ~ ACTION ~ REWARD

PLAN   Write down the things you choose to ACHIEVE TODAY

ACTION   Write down THE TASKS to achieve your plan

REWARD   Write down how you will REWARD yourself for completing your plan

WRITE 1 POSITIVE BELIEF ABOUT YOURSELF BELOW:

QUOTE OF THE DAY
Shift your mindset to lift your life

18

POSITIVITY

Write down something negative you experienced today - then under it list the positives you can take out of that experience

SELF LOVE

What activities have you done to nurture your love for yourself?

DOWNTIME / CHILL

What did you do to chill out today or to wind down and give yourself a break?

HOW HAPPY DID YOU FEEL TODAY?

 0   1   2   3   4   😔   6   7   8   9   10   😄

USE ONE WORD TO DESCRIBE HOW YOU ARE FEELING:

WHAT DID YOU DO THAT WAS FUN TODAY?

ENERGY

WHAT'S BEEN DRAINING YOUR ENERGY TODAY?

WHAT'S BOOSTED YOUR ENERGY TODAY?

STRESS

WHAT'S ADDED TO THE STRESS IN YOUR DAY?

WHAT'S HELPED TO REDUCE YOUR STRESS TODAY?

DAY 3

AM

DATE:

Fill in 3 daily affirmations to keep your energy positive and build yourself up & 3 things you are grateful for.
Finally write out your daily manifestation for what you choose to bring into your life, with gratitude and feeling
as if you already have it now (your manifestation may be the same as the day before but it's important to write it out).

AFFIRMATIONS	GRATITUDE	DAILY MANIFESTATION
# 1	# 1	
# 2	# 2	
# 3	# 3	

PLAN ~ ACTION ~ REWARD

PLAN Write down the things you choose to ACHIEVE TODAY

ACTION Write down THE TASKS to achieve your plan

REWARD Write down how you will REWARD yourself for completing your plan

WRITE 1 POSITIVE BELIEF ABOUT YOURSELF BELOW:

QUOTE OF THE DAY

The more you practice the easier it will become

POSITIVITY

Write down something negative you experienced today - then under it list the positives you can take out of that experience

SELF LOVE

What activities have you done to nurture your love for yourself?

DOWNTIME / CHILL

What did you do to chill out today or to wind down and give yourself a break?

HOW HAPPY DID YOU FEEL TODAY?

 0   1   2   3   4   😑   6   7   8   9   10   😄

USE ONE WORD TO DESCRIBE HOW YOU ARE FEELING:

WHAT DID YOU DO THAT WAS FUN TODAY?

ENERGY

WHAT'S BEEN DRAINING YOUR
ENERGY TODAY?

WHAT'S BOOSTED YOUR
ENERGY TODAY?

STRESS

WHAT'S ADDED TO THE STRESS
IN YOUR DAY?

WHAT'S HELPED TO REDUCE
YOUR STRESS TODAY?

DAY 4

AM

DATE:

Fill in 3 daily affirmations to keep your energy positive and build yourself up & 3 things you are grateful for.
Finally write out your daily manifestation for what you choose to bring into your life, with gratitude and feeling
as if you already have it now (your manifestation may be the same as the day before but it's important to write it out).

AFFIRMATIONS	GRATITUDE	DAILY MANIFESTATION
# 1	# 1	
# 2	# 2	
# 3	# 3	

PLAN ~ ACTION ~ REWARD

PLAN   Write down the things you choose to ACHIEVE TODAY

ACTION   Write down THE TASKS to achieve your plan

REWARD   Write down how you will REWARD yourself for completing your plan

 👍👎   👍👎   👍👎   👍👎   ⭐⭐⭐☆☆ 👍👎   👍👎

 WRITE 1 POSITIVE BELIEF ABOUT YOURSELF BELOW:

QUOTE OF THE DAY
*What you Resist the most is often what
you Need the most*

PM

POSITIVITY

Write down something negative you experienced today - then under it list the positives you can take out of that experience

SELF LOVE

What activities have you done to nurture your love for yourself?

DOWNTIME / CHILL

What did you do to chill out today or to wind down and give yourself a break?

HOW HAPPY DID YOU FEEL TODAY?

 0   1   2   3   4   6   7   8   9   10   😄

USE ONE WORD TO DESCRIBE HOW YOU ARE FEELING:

WHAT DID YOU DO THAT WAS FUN TODAY?

ENERGY

WHAT'S BEEN DRAINING YOUR ENERGY TODAY?

WHAT'S BOOSTED YOUR ENERGY TODAY?

STRESS

WHAT'S ADDED TO THE STRESS IN YOUR DAY?

WHAT'S HELPED TO REDUCE YOUR STRESS TODAY?

Fill in 3 daily affirmations to keep your energy positive and build yourself up & 3 things you are grateful for.
Finally write out your daily manifestation for what you choose to bring into your life, with gratitude and feeling
as if you already have it now (your manifestation may be the same as the day before but it's important to write it out).

AFFIRMATIONS	GRATITUDE	DAILY MANIFESTATION
# 1	# 1	
# 2	# 2	
# 3	# 3	

PLAN ~ ACTION ~ REWARD

PLAN Write down the things you choose to ACHIEVE TODAY

ACTION Write down THE TASKS to achieve your plan

REWARD Write down how you will REWARD yourself for completing your plan

WRITE 1 POSITIVE BELIEF ABOUT YOURSELF BELOW:

QUOTE OF THE DAY

You're in the driver's seat of your life

POSITIVITY

Write down something negative you experienced today - then under it list the positives you can take out of that experience

SELF LOVE

What activities have you done to nurture your love for yourself?

DOWNTIME / CHILL

What did you do to chill out today or to wind down and give yourself a break?

HOW HAPPY DID YOU FEEL TODAY?

 0   1   2   3   4   😔   6   7   8   9   10   😄

USE ONE WORD TO DESCRIBE HOW YOU ARE FEELING:

WHAT DID YOU DO THAT WAS FUN TODAY?

ENERGY

WHAT'S BEEN DRAINING YOUR
ENERGY TODAY?

WHAT'S BOOSTED YOUR
ENERGY TODAY?

STRESS

WHAT'S ADDED TO THE STRESS
IN YOUR DAY?

WHAT'S HELPED TO REDUCE
YOUR STRESS TODAY?

DAY 6

AM

DATE:

Fill in 3 daily affirmations to keep your energy positive and build yourself up & 3 things you are grateful for.
Finally write out your daily manifestation for what you choose to bring into your life, with gratitude and feeling
as if you already have it now (your manifestation may be the same as the day before but it's important to write it out).

AFFIRMATIONS	GRATITUDE	DAILY MANIFESTATION
# 1	# 1	
# 2	# 2	
# 3	# 3	

PLAN ~ ACTION ~ REWARD

PLAN   Write down the things you choose to ACHIEVE TODAY

ACTION   Write down THE TASKS to achieve your plan

REWARD   Write down how you will REWARD yourself for completing your plan

WRITE 1 POSITIVE BELIEF ABOUT YOURSELF BELOW:

QUOTE OF THE DAY

Your thoughts become your Reality

POSITIVITY

Write down something negative you experienced today - then under it list the positives you can take out of that experience

SELF LOVE

What activities have you done to nurture your love for yourself?

DOWNTIME / CHILL

What did you do to chill out today or to wind down and give yourself a break?

HOW HAPPY DID YOU FEEL TODAY?

  0   1   2   3   4   6   7   8   9   10 😄

USE ONE WORD TO DESCRIBE HOW YOU ARE FEELING:

WHAT DID YOU DO THAT WAS FUN TODAY?

ENERGY

WHAT'S BEEN DRAINING YOUR
ENERGY TODAY?

WHAT'S BOOSTED YOUR
ENERGY TODAY?

STRESS

WHAT'S ADDED TO THE STRESS
IN YOUR DAY?

WHAT'S HELPED TO REDUCE
YOUR STRESS TODAY?

DAY 7

AM

DATE:

Fill in 3 daily affirmations to keep your energy positive and build yourself up & 3 things you are grateful for.
Finally write out your daily manifestation for what you choose to bring into your life, with gratitude and feeling
as if you already have it now (your manifestation may be the same as the day before but it's important to write it out).

AFFIRMATIONS	GRATITUDE	DAILY MANIFESTATION
# 1	# 1	
# 2	# 2	
# 3	# 3	

PLAN ~ ACTION ~ REWARD

PLAN Write down the things you choose to ACHIEVE TODAY

ACTION Write down THE TASKS to achieve your plan

REWARD Write down how you will REWARD yourself for completing your plan

WRITE 1 POSITIVE BELIEF ABOUT YOURSELF BELOW:

QUOTE OF THE DAY
Surround yourself with like minded people

PM

POSITIVITY

Write down something negative you experienced today - then under it list the positives you can take out of that experience

SELF LOVE

What activities have you done to nurture your love for yourself?

DOWNTIME / CHILL

What did you do to chill out today or to wind down and give yourself a break?

HOW HAPPY DID YOU FEEL TODAY?

0   1   2   3   4   (5)   6   7   8   9   10   😄

USE ONE WORD TO DESCRIBE HOW YOU ARE FEELING:

WHAT DID YOU DO THAT WAS FUN TODAY?

ENERGY

WHAT'S BEEN DRAINING YOUR
ENERGY TODAY?

WHAT'S BOOSTED YOUR
ENERGY TODAY?

STRESS

WHAT'S ADDED TO THE STRESS
IN YOUR DAY?

WHAT'S HELPED TO REDUCE
YOUR STRESS TODAY?

WEEKLY CHECK-IN
IT'S TIME TO REFLECT AND ASSESS ON THE PAST WEEK
Getting to know yourself takes time, it's all about small steps & growing each week.

Starting with the positive, what have you enjoyed about your past week?

Where did you succeed, what were your wins and did you celebrate them?

What did you struggle with, what was your biggest challenge, what stopped you from achieving your plan and goals?

What are you aiming to improve upon in the coming week?

What is your intention for the coming week?

DAY 8

DATE:

Fill in 3 daily affirmations to keep your energy positive and build yourself up & 3 things you are grateful for.
Finally write out your daily manifestation for what you choose to bring into your life, with gratitude and feeling
as if you already have it now (your manifestation may be the same as the day before but it's important to write it out).

AFFIRMATIONS	GRATITUDE	DAILY MANIFESTATION
# 1	# 1	
# 2	# 2	
# 3	# 3	

PLAN ~ ACTION ~ REWARD

PLAN Write down the things you choose to ACHIEVE TODAY

ACTION Write down THE TASKS to achieve your plan

REWARD Write down how you will REWARD yourself for completing your plan

WRITE 1 POSITIVE BELIEF ABOUT YOURSELF BELOW:

QUOTE OF THE DAY

This is your Life — your journey — so consciously create a FUN & Joyful one

POSITIVITY

Write down something negative you experienced today - then under it list the positives you can take out of that experience

SELF LOVE

What activities have you done to nurture your love for yourself?

DOWNTIME / CHILL

What did you do to chill out today or to wind down and give yourself a break?

HOW HAPPY DID YOU FEEL TODAY?

  0   1   2   3   4   6   7   8   9   10 😄

USE ONE WORD TO DESCRIBE HOW YOU ARE FEELING:

WHAT DID YOU DO THAT WAS FUN TODAY?

ENERGY

WHAT'S BEEN DRAINING YOUR ENERGY TODAY?

WHAT'S BOOSTED YOUR ENERGY TODAY?

STRESS

WHAT'S ADDED TO THE STRESS IN YOUR DAY?

WHAT'S HELPED TO REDUCE YOUR STRESS TODAY?

33

AM

DATE:

Fill in 3 daily affirmations to keep your energy positive and build yourself up & 3 things you are grateful for. Finally write out your daily manifestation for what you choose to bring into your life, with gratitude and feeling as if you already have it now (your manifestation may be the same as the day before but it's important to write it out).

AFFIRMATIONS	GRATITUDE	DAILY MANIFESTATION
# 1	# 1	
# 2	# 2	
# 3	# 3	

PLAN ~ ACTION ~ REWARD

PLAN   Write down the things you choose to ACHIEVE TODAY

ACTION   Write down THE TASKS to achieve your plan

REWARD   Write down how you will REWARD yourself for completing your plan

WRITE 1 POSITIVE BELIEF ABOUT YOURSELF BELOW:

QUOTE OF THE DAY

Let it go and just say No

POSITIVITY

Write down something negative you experienced today - then under it list the positives you can take out of that experience

SELF LOVE

What activities have you done to nurture your love for yourself?

DOWNTIME / CHILL

What did you do to chill out today or to wind down and give yourself a break?

HOW HAPPY DID YOU FEEL TODAY?

  0   1   2   3   4   6   7   8   9   10   😄

USE ONE WORD TO DESCRIBE HOW YOU ARE FEELING:

-

WHAT DID YOU DO THAT WAS FUN TODAY?

ENERGY

WHAT'S BEEN DRAINING YOUR ENERGY TODAY?

WHAT'S BOOSTED YOUR ENERGY TODAY?

STRESS

WHAT'S ADDED TO THE STRESS IN YOUR DAY?

WHAT'S HELPED TO REDUCE YOUR STRESS TODAY?

DAY 10

AM

DATE:

Fill in 3 daily affirmations to keep your energy positive and build yourself up & 3 things you are grateful for.
Finally write out your daily manifestation for what you choose to bring into your life, with gratitude and feeling
as if you already have it now (your manifestation may be the same as the day before but it's important to write it out).

AFFIRMATIONS	GRATITUDE	DAILY MANIFESTATION
# 1	# 1	
# 2	# 2	
# 3	# 3	

PLAN ~ ACTION ~ REWARD

PLAN   Write down the things you choose to ACHIEVE TODAY

ACTION   Write down THE TASKS to achieve your plan

REWARD   Write down how you will REWARD yourself for completing your plan

WRITE 1 POSITIVE BELIEF ABOUT YOURSELF BELOW:

QUOTE OF THE DAY
Get your mind Right and everything else follows

36

POSITIVITY

Write down something negative you experienced today - then under it list the positives you can take out of that experience

SELF LOVE

What activities have you done to nurture your love for yourself?

DOWNTIME / CHILL

What did you do to chill out today or to wind down and give yourself a break?

HOW HAPPY DID YOU FEEL TODAY?

 0   1   2   3   4   😔   6   7   8   9   10   😄

USE ONE WORD TO DESCRIBE HOW YOU ARE FEELING:

WHAT DID YOU DO THAT WAS FUN TODAY?

ENERGY

WHAT'S BEEN DRAINING YOUR ENERGY TODAY?

WHAT'S BOOSTED YOUR ENERGY TODAY?

STRESS

WHAT'S ADDED TO THE STRESS IN YOUR DAY?

WHAT'S HELPED TO REDUCE YOUR STRESS TODAY?

DAY 11

AM

DATE:

Fill in 3 daily affirmations to keep your energy positive and build yourself up & 3 things you are grateful for.
Finally write out your daily manifestation for what you choose to bring into your life, with gratitude and feeling
as if you already have it now (your manifestation may be the same as the day before but it's important to write it out).

AFFIRMATIONS	GRATITUDE	DAILY MANIFESTATION
# 1	# 1	
# 2	# 2	
# 3	# 3	

PLAN ~ ACTION ~ REWARD

PLAN   Write down the things you choose to ACHIEVE TODAY

ACTION   Write down THE TASKS to achieve your plan

REWARD   Write down how you will REWARD yourself for completing your plan

WRITE 1 POSITIVE BELIEF ABOUT YOURSELF BELOW:

QUOTE OF THE DAY
Trust & believe in yourself

POSITIVITY

Write down something negative you experienced today - then under it list the positives you can take out of that experience

SELF LOVE

What activities have you done to nurture your love for yourself?

DOWNTIME / CHILL

What did you do to chill out today or to wind down and give yourself a break?

HOW HAPPY DID YOU FEEL TODAY?

  0   1   2   3   4   6   7   8   9   10   😄

USE ONE WORD TO DESCRIBE HOW YOU ARE FEELING:

WHAT DID YOU DO THAT WAS FUN TODAY?

ENERGY

WHAT'S BEEN DRAINING YOUR ENERGY TODAY?

WHAT'S BOOSTED YOUR ENERGY TODAY?

STRESS

WHAT'S ADDED TO THE STRESS IN YOUR DAY?

WHAT'S HELPED TO REDUCE YOUR STRESS TODAY?

DAY 12

DATE:

Fill in 3 daily affirmations to keep your energy positive and build yourself up & 3 things you are grateful for.
Finally write out your daily manifestation for what you choose to bring into your life, with gratitude and feeling
as if you already have it now (your manifestation may be the same as the day before but it's important to write it out).

AFFIRMATIONS	GRATITUDE	DAILY MANIFESTATION
# 1	# 1	
# 2	# 2	
# 3	# 3	

PLAN ~ ACTION ~ REWARD

PLAN   Write down the things you choose to ACHIEVE TODAY

ACTION   Write down THE TASKS to achieve your plan

REWARD   Write down how you will REWARD yourself for completing your plan

WRITE 1 POSITIVE BELIEF ABOUT YOURSELF BELOW:

QUOTE OF THE DAY
Manifest your destiny

POSITIVITY

Write down something negative you experienced today - then under it list the positives you can take out of that experience

SELF LOVE ·

What activities have you done to nurture your love for yourself?

DOWNTIME / CHILL

What did you do to chill out today or to wind down and give yourself a break?

HOW HAPPY DID YOU FEEL TODAY?

 0 1 2 3 4 5 6 7 8 9 10 😄

USE ONE WORD TO DESCRIBE HOW YOU ARE FEELING:

WHAT DID YOU DO THAT WAS FUN TODAY?

ENERGY

WHAT'S BEEN DRAINING YOUR ENERGY TODAY?

WHAT'S BOOSTED YOUR ENERGY TODAY?

STRESS

WHAT'S ADDED TO THE STRESS IN YOUR DAY?

WHAT'S HELPED TO REDUCE YOUR STRESS TODAY?

DAY 13

DATE:

Fill in 3 daily affirmations to keep your energy positive and build yourself up & 3 things you are grateful for.
Finally write out your daily manifestation for what you choose to bring into your life, with gratitude and feeling
as if you already have it now (your manifestation may be the same as the day before but it's important to write it out).

AFFIRMATIONS	GRATITUDE	DAILY MANIFESTATION
# 1	# 1	
# 2	# 2	
# 3	# 3	

PLAN ~ ACTION ~ REWARD

PLAN   Write down the things you choose to ACHIEVE TODAY

ACTION   Write down THE TASKS to achieve your plan

REWARD   Write down how you will REWARD yourself for completing your plan

WRITE 1 POSITIVE BELIEF ABOUT YOURSELF BELOW:

QUOTE OF THE DAY

Love yourself first

42

PM

POSITIVITY

Write down something negative you experienced today - then under it list the positives you can take out of that experience

SELF LOVE

What activities have you done to nurture your love for yourself?

DOWNTIME / CHILL

What did you do to chill out today or to wind down and give yourself a break?

HOW HAPPY DID YOU FEEL TODAY?

 0   1   2   3   4   😔   6   7   8   9   10   😄

USE ONE WORD TO DESCRIBE HOW YOU ARE FEELING:

WHAT DID YOU DO THAT WAS FUN TODAY?

ENERGY

WHAT'S BEEN DRAINING YOUR
ENERGY TODAY?

WHAT'S BOOSTED YOUR
ENERGY TODAY?

STRESS

WHAT'S ADDED TO THE STRESS
IN YOUR DAY?

WHAT'S HELPED TO REDUCE
YOUR STRESS TODAY?

DAY 14

 AM

DATE:

Fill in 3 daily affirmations to keep your energy positive and build yourself up & 3 things you are grateful for.
Finally write out your daily manifestation for what you choose to bring into your life, with gratitude and feeling
as if you already have it now (your manifestation may be the same as the day before but it's important to write it out).

AFFIRMATIONS	GRATITUDE	DAILY MANIFESTATION
# 1	# 1	
# 2	# 2	
# 3	# 3	

PLAN ~ ACTION ~ REWARD

PLAN   Write down the things you choose to ACHIEVE TODAY

ACTION   Write down THE TASKS to achieve your plan

REWARD   Write down how you will REWARD yourself for completing your plan

 WRITE 1 POSITIVE BELIEF ABOUT YOURSELF BELOW:

QUOTE OF THE DAY

You learn more from failure than from success

PM

POSITIVITY
Write down something negative you experienced today - then under it list the positives you can take out of that experience

SELF LOVE
What activities have you done to nurture your love for yourself?

DOWNTIME / CHILL
What did you do to chill out today or to wind down and give yourself a break?

HOW HAPPY DID YOU FEEL TODAY?

 0   1   2   3   4   6   7   8   9   10   😄

USE ONE WORD TO DESCRIBE HOW YOU ARE FEELING:

WHAT DID YOU DO THAT WAS FUN TODAY?

ENERGY

WHAT'S BEEN DRAINING YOUR ENERGY TODAY?

WHAT'S BOOSTED YOUR ENERGY TODAY?

STRESS

WHAT'S ADDED TO THE STRESS IN YOUR DAY?

WHAT'S HELPED TO REDUCE YOUR STRESS TODAY?

WEEKLY CHECK-IN
IT'S TIME TO REFLECT AND ASSESS ON THE PAST WEEK

Getting to know yourself takes time, it's all about small steps & growing each week.

Starting with the positive, what have you enjoyed about your past week?

Where did you succeed, what were your wins and did you celebrate them?

What did you struggle with, what was your biggest challenge, what stopped you from achieving your plan and goals?

What are you aiming to improve upon in the coming week?

What is your intention for the coming week?

AM

DATE:

Fill in 3 daily affirmations to keep your energy positive and build yourself up & 3 things you are grateful for. Finally write out your daily manifestation for what you choose to bring into your life, with gratitude and feeling as if you already have it now (your manifestation may be the same as the day before but it's important to write it out).

AFFIRMATIONS	GRATITUDE	DAILY MANIFESTATION
# 1	# 1	
# 2	# 2	
# 3	# 3	

PLAN ~ ACTION ~ REWARD

PLAN   Write down the things you choose to ACHIEVE TODAY

ACTION   Write down THE TASKS to achieve your plan

REWARD   Write down how you will REWARD yourself for completing your plan

WRITE 1 POSITIVE BELIEF ABOUT YOURSELF BELOW:

QUOTE OF THE DAY

Positivity and Gratitude Knock Negativity and self sabotage out of the park

POSITIVITY

Write down something negative you experienced today - then under it list the positives you can take out of that experience

SELF LOVE

What activities have you done to nurture your love for yourself?

DOWNTIME / CHILL

What did you do to chill out today or to wind down and give yourself a break?

HOW HAPPY DID YOU FEEL TODAY?

 0 1 2 3 4 5 6 7 8 9 10

USE ONE WORD TO DESCRIBE HOW YOU ARE FEELING:

WHAT DID YOU DO THAT WAS FUN TODAY?

ENERGY

WHAT'S BEEN DRAINING YOUR ENERGY TODAY?

WHAT'S BOOSTED YOUR ENERGY TODAY?

STRESS

WHAT'S ADDED TO THE STRESS IN YOUR DAY?

WHAT'S HELPED TO REDUCE YOUR STRESS TODAY?

DAY 16

DATE:

Fill in 3 daily affirmations to keep your energy positive and build yourself up & 3 things you are grateful for.
Finally write out your daily manifestation for what you choose to bring into your life, with gratitude and feeling
as if you already have it now (your manifestation may be the same as the day before but it's important to write it out).

AFFIRMATIONS	GRATITUDE	DAILY MANIFESTATION
# 1	# 1	
# 2	# 2	
# 3	# 3	

PLAN ~ ACTION ~ REWARD

PLAN   Write down the things you choose to ACHIEVE TODAY

ACTION   Write down THE TASKS to achieve your plan

REWARD   Write down how you will REWARD yourself for completing your plan

WRITE 1 POSITIVE BELIEF ABOUT YOURSELF BELOW:

QUOTE OF THE DAY
Create positive change in your life

POSITIVITY

Write down something negative you experienced today - then under it list the positives you can take out of that experience

SELF LOVE

What activities have you done to nurture your love for yourself?

DOWNTIME / CHILL

What did you do to chill out today or to wind down and give yourself a break?

HOW HAPPY DID YOU FEEL TODAY?

 0   1   2   3   4   😐   6   7   8   9   10   😄

USE ONE WORD TO DESCRIBE HOW YOU ARE FEELING:

WHAT DID YOU DO THAT WAS FUN TODAY?

ENERGY

WHAT'S BEEN DRAINING YOUR ENERGY TODAY?

WHAT'S BOOSTED YOUR ENERGY TODAY?

STRESS

WHAT'S ADDED TO THE STRESS IN YOUR DAY?

WHAT'S HELPED TO REDUCE YOUR STRESS TODAY?

DAY 17 AM

DATE:

Fill in 3 daily affirmations to keep your energy positive and build yourself up & 3 things you are grateful for.
Finally write out your daily manifestation for what you choose to bring into your life, with gratitude and feeling
as if you already have it now (your manifestation may be the same as the day before but it's important to write it out).

AFFIRMATIONS	GRATITUDE	DAILY MANIFESTATION
# 1	# 1	
# 2	# 2	
# 3	# 3	

PLAN ~ ACTION ~ REWARD

PLAN　　　Write down the things you choose to ACHIEVE TODAY

ACTION　　Write down THE TASKS to achieve your plan

REWARD　　Write down how you will REWARD yourself for completing your plan

 WRITE 1 POSITIVE BELIEF ABOUT YOURSELF BELOW:

QUOTE OF THE DAY
There's nothing more attractive than confidence

POSITIVITY

*Write down something negative you
experienced today - then under it list the
positives you can take out of that experience*

SELF LOVE

*What activities have you done to nurture
your love for yourself?*

DOWNTIME / CHILL

*What did you do to chill out today or to wind
down and give yourself a break?*

HOW HAPPY DID YOU FEEL TODAY?

   0   1   2   3   4   😔   6   7   8   9   10   😄

USE ONE WORD TO DESCRIBE HOW YOU ARE FEELING:

WHAT DID YOU DO THAT WAS FUN TODAY?

ENERGY

WHAT'S BEEN DRAINING YOUR
ENERGY TODAY?

WHAT'S BOOSTED YOUR
ENERGY TODAY?

STRESS

WHAT'S ADDED TO THE STRESS
IN YOUR DAY?

WHAT'S HELPED TO REDUCE
YOUR STRESS TODAY?

DAY 18

AM

DATE:

Fill in 3 daily affirmations to keep your energy positive and build yourself up & 3 things you are grateful for.
Finally write out your daily manifestation for what you choose to bring into your life, with gratitude and feeling
as if you already have it now (your manifestation may be the same as the day before but it's important to write it out).

AFFIRMATIONS	GRATITUDE	DAILY MANIFESTATION
# 1	# 1	
# 2	# 2	
# 3	# 3	

PLAN ~ ACTION ~ REWARD

PLAN Write down the things you choose to ACHIEVE TODAY

ACTION Write down THE TASKS to achieve your plan

REWARD Write down how you will REWARD yourself for completing your plan

WRITE 1 POSITIVE BELIEF ABOUT YOURSELF BELOW:

QUOTE OF THE DAY
Get comfortable with being uncomfortable –
this is when change happens

54

POSITIVITY

Write down something negative you experienced today - then under it list the positives you can take out of that experience

SELF LOVE

What activities have you done to nurture your love for yourself?

DOWNTIME / CHILL

What did you do to chill out today or to wind down and give yourself a break?

HOW HAPPY DID YOU FEEL TODAY?

  0   1   2   3   4   😐   6   7   8   9   10   😄

USE ONE WORD TO DESCRIBE HOW YOU ARE FEELING:

WHAT DID YOU DO THAT WAS FUN TODAY?

ENERGY

WHAT'S BEEN DRAINING YOUR ENERGY TODAY?

WHAT'S BOOSTED YOUR ENERGY TODAY?

STRESS

WHAT'S ADDED TO THE STRESS IN YOUR DAY?

WHAT'S HELPED TO REDUCE YOUR STRESS TODAY?

AM

Fill in 3 daily affirmations to keep your energy positive and build yourself up & 3 things you are grateful for.
Finally write out your daily manifestation for what you choose to bring into your life, with gratitude and feeling
as if you already have it now (your manifestation may be the same as the day before but it's important to write it out).

AFFIRMATIONS	GRATITUDE	DAILY MANIFESTATION
# 1	# 1	
# 2	# 2	
# 3	# 3	

PLAN ~ ACTION ~ REWARD

PLAN Write down the things you choose to ACHIEVE TODAY

ACTION Write down THE TASKS to achieve your plan

REWARD Write down how you will REWARD yourself for completing your plan

WRITE 1 POSITIVE BELIEF ABOUT YOURSELF BELOW:

QUOTE OF THE DAY

You are capable of greatness

POSITIVITY

Write down something negative you experienced today - then under it list the positives you can take out of that experience

SELF LOVE

What activities have you done to nurture your love for yourself?

DOWNTIME / CHILL

What did you do to chill out today or to wind down and give yourself a break?

HOW HAPPY DID YOU FEEL TODAY?

 0   1   2   3   4   😐   6   7   8   9   10   😄

USE ONE WORD TO DESCRIBE HOW YOU ARE FEELING:

WHAT DID YOU DO THAT WAS FUN TODAY?

ENERGY

WHAT'S BEEN DRAINING YOUR ENERGY TODAY?

WHAT'S BOOSTED YOUR ENERGY TODAY?

STRESS

WHAT'S ADDED TO THE STRESS IN YOUR DAY?

WHAT'S HELPED TO REDUCE YOUR STRESS TODAY?

DAY 20

AM

DATE:

Fill in 3 daily affirmations to keep your energy positive and build yourself up & 3 things you are grateful for. Finally write out your daily manifestation for what you choose to bring into your life, with gratitude and feeling as if you already have it now (your manifestation may be the same as the day before but it's important to write it out).

AFFIRMATIONS	GRATITUDE	DAILY MANIFESTATION
# 1	# 1	
# 2	# 2	
# 3	# 3	

PLAN ~ ACTION ~ REWARD

PLAN   Write down the things you choose to ACHIEVE TODAY

ACTION   Write down THE TASKS to achieve your plan

REWARD   Write down how you will REWARD yourself for completing your plan

WRITE 1 POSITIVE BELIEF ABOUT YOURSELF BELOW:

QUOTE OF THE DAY
Have attitude with Gratitude

58

POSITIVITY

Write down something negative you experienced today - then under it list the positives you can take out of that experience

SELF LOVE

What activities have you done to nurture your love for yourself?

DOWNTIME / CHILL

What did you do to chill out today or to wind down and give yourself a break?

HOW HAPPY DID YOU FEEL TODAY?

 0   1   2   3   4   😐   6   7   8   9   10   😄

USE ONE WORD TO DESCRIBE HOW YOU ARE FEELING:

WHAT DID YOU DO THAT WAS FUN TODAY?

ENERGY

WHAT'S BEEN DRAINING YOUR ENERGY TODAY?

WHAT'S BOOSTED YOUR ENERGY TODAY?

STRESS

WHAT'S ADDED TO THE STRESS IN YOUR DAY?

WHAT'S HELPED TO REDUCE YOUR STRESS TODAY?

DAY 21

 AM

DATE:

Fill in 3 daily affirmations to keep your energy positive and build yourself up & 3 things you are grateful for.
Finally write out your daily manifestation for what you choose to bring into your life, with gratitude and feeling
as if you already have it now (your manifestation may be the same as the day before but it's important to write it out).

AFFIRMATIONS	GRATITUDE	DAILY MANIFESTATION
# 1	# 1	
# 2	# 2	
# 3	# 3	

PLAN ~ ACTION ~ REWARD

PLAN   Write down the things you choose to ACHIEVE TODAY

ACTION   Write down THE TASKS to achieve your plan

REWARD   Write down how you will REWARD yourself for completing your plan

 WRITE 1 POSITIVE BELIEF ABOUT YOURSELF BELOW:

QUOTE OF THE DAY
Let shit go and it will flow

POSITIVITY

Write down something negative you experienced today - then under it list the positives you can take out of that experience

SELF LOVE

What activities have you done to nurture your love for yourself?

DOWNTIME / CHILL

What did you do to chill out today or to wind down and give yourself a break?

HOW HAPPY DID YOU FEEL TODAY?

 0   1   2   3   4   6   7   8   9   10   😄

USE ONE WORD TO DESCRIBE HOW YOU ARE FEELING:

WHAT DID YOU DO THAT WAS FUN TODAY?

ENERGY

WHAT'S BEEN DRAINING YOUR ENERGY TODAY?

WHAT'S BOOSTED YOUR ENERGY TODAY?

STRESS

WHAT'S ADDED TO THE STRESS IN YOUR DAY?

WHAT'S HELPED TO REDUCE YOUR STRESS TODAY?

WEEKLY CHECK-IN
IT'S TIME TO REFLECT AND ASSESS ON THE PAST WEEK
Getting to know yourself takes time, it's all about small steps & growing each week.

Starting with the positive, what have you enjoyed about your past week?

Where did you succeed, what were your wins and did you celebrate them?

What did you struggle with, what was your biggest challenge, what stopped you from achieving your plan and goals?

What are you aiming to improve upon in the coming week?

What is your intention for the coming week?

DAY 22

DATE:

Fill in 3 daily affirmations to keep your energy positive and build yourself up & 3 things you are grateful for.
Finally write out your daily manifestation for what you choose to bring into your life, with gratitude and feeling
as if you already have it now (your manifestation may be the same as the day before but it's important to write it out).

AFFIRMATIONS	GRATITUDE	DAILY MANIFESTATION
# 1	# 1	
# 2	# 2	
# 3	# 3	

PLAN ~ ACTION ~ REWARD

PLAN Write down the things you choose to ACHIEVE TODAY

ACTION Write down THE TASKS to achieve your plan

REWARD Write down how you will REWARD yourself for completing your plan

WRITE 1 POSITIVE BELIEF ABOUT YOURSELF BELOW:

QUOTE OF THE DAY
Start with simple small steps

POSITIVITY

Write down something negative you experienced today - then under it list the positives you can take out of that experience

SELF LOVE

What activities have you done to nurture your love for yourself?

DOWNTIME / CHILL

What did you do to chill out today or to wind down and give yourself a break?

HOW HAPPY DID YOU FEEL TODAY?

 0   1   2   3   4   😐   6   7   8   9   10   😄

USE ONE WORD TO DESCRIBE HOW YOU ARE FEELING:

WHAT DID YOU DO THAT WAS FUN TODAY?

ENERGY

WHAT'S BEEN DRAINING YOUR ENERGY TODAY?

WHAT'S BOOSTED YOUR ENERGY TODAY?

STRESS

WHAT'S ADDED TO THE STRESS IN YOUR DAY?

WHAT'S HELPED TO REDUCE YOUR STRESS TODAY?

DAY 23

 AM

DATE:

Fill in 3 daily affirmations to keep your energy positive and build yourself up & 3 things you are grateful for.
Finally write out your daily manifestation for what you choose to bring into your life, with gratitude and feeling
as if you already have it now (your manifestation may be the same as the day before but it's important to write it out).

AFFIRMATIONS	GRATITUDE	DAILY MANIFESTATION
# 1	# 1	
# 2	# 2	
# 3	# 3	

PLAN ~ ACTION ~ REWARD

PLAN   Write down the things you choose to ACHIEVE TODAY

ACTION   Write down THE TASKS to achieve your plan

REWARD   Write down how you will REWARD yourself for completing your plan

WRITE 1 POSITIVE BELIEF ABOUT YOURSELF BELOW:

QUOTE OF THE DAY

wake up! It's your turn to fly

66

POSITIVITY

Write down something negative you experienced today - then under it list the positives you can take out of that experience

SELF LOVE

What activities have you done to nurture your love for yourself?

DOWNTIME / CHILL

What did you do to chill out today or to wind down and give yourself a break?

HOW HAPPY DID YOU FEEL TODAY?

  0   1   2   3   4   6   7   8   9   10   😄

USE ONE WORD TO DESCRIBE HOW YOU ARE FEELING:

WHAT DID YOU DO THAT WAS FUN TODAY?

ENERGY

WHAT'S BEEN DRAINING YOUR
ENERGY TODAY?

WHAT'S BOOSTED YOUR
ENERGY TODAY?

STRESS

WHAT'S ADDED TO THE STRESS
IN YOUR DAY?

WHAT'S HELPED TO REDUCE
YOUR STRESS TODAY?

AM DATE:

Fill in 3 daily affirmations to keep your energy positive and build yourself up & 3 things you are grateful for.
Finally write out your daily manifestation for what you choose to bring into your life, with gratitude and feeling
as if you already have it now (your manifestation may be the same as the day before but it's important to write it out).

AFFIRMATIONS	GRATITUDE	DAILY MANIFESTATION
# 1	# 1	
# 2	# 2	
# 3	# 3	

PLAN ~ ACTION ~ REWARD

PLAN Write down the things you choose to ACHIEVE TODAY

ACTION Write down THE TASKS to achieve your plan

REWARD Write down how you will REWARD yourself for completing your plan

WRITE 1 POSITIVE BELIEF ABOUT YOURSELF BELOW:

QUOTE OF THE DAY
Empower Yourself Inside and out

POSITIVITY

Write down something negative you experienced today - then under it list the positives you can take out of that experience

SELF LOVE

What activities have you done to nurture your love for yourself?

DOWNTIME / CHILL

What did you do to chill out today or to wind down and give yourself a break?

HOW HAPPY DID YOU FEEL TODAY?

 0   1   2   3   4   (😔)   6   7   8   9   10   (😄)

USE ONE WORD TO DESCRIBE HOW YOU ARE FEELING:

WHAT DID YOU DO THAT WAS FUN TODAY?

ENERGY

WHAT'S BEEN DRAINING YOUR ENERGY TODAY?

WHAT'S BOOSTED YOUR ENERGY TODAY?

STRESS

WHAT'S ADDED TO THE STRESS IN YOUR DAY?

WHAT'S HELPED TO REDUCE YOUR STRESS TODAY?

AM

DATE:

Fill in 3 daily affirmations to keep your energy positive and build yourself up & 3 things you are grateful for.
Finally write out your daily manifestation for what you choose to bring into your life, with gratitude and feeling
as if you already have it now (your manifestation may be the same as the day before but it's important to write it out).

AFFIRMATIONS	GRATITUDE	DAILY MANIFESTATION
# 1	# 1	
# 2	# 2	
# 3	# 3	

PLAN ~ ACTION ~ REWARD

PLAN Write down the things you choose to ACHIEVE TODAY

ACTION Write down THE TASKS to achieve your plan

REWARD Write down how you will REWARD yourself for completing your plan

WRITE 1 POSITIVE BELIEF ABOUT YOURSELF BELOW:

QUOTE OF THE DAY

Step into your authentic self and watch yourself grow

POSITIVITY

Write down something negative you experienced today - then under it list the positives you can take out of that experience

SELF LOVE

What activities have you done to nurture your love for yourself?

DOWNTIME / CHILL

What did you do to chill out today or to wind down and give yourself a break?

HOW HAPPY DID YOU FEEL TODAY?

  0   1   2   3   4   6   7   8   9   10 😄

USE ONE WORD TO DESCRIBE HOW YOU ARE FEELING:

WHAT DID YOU DO THAT WAS FUN TODAY?

ENERGY

WHAT'S BEEN DRAINING YOUR
ENERGY TODAY?

WHAT'S BOOSTED YOUR
ENERGY TODAY?

STRESS

WHAT'S ADDED TO THE STRESS
IN YOUR DAY?

WHAT'S HELPED TO REDUCE
YOUR STRESS TODAY?

Fill in 3 daily affirmations to keep your energy positive and build yourself up & 3 things you are grateful for.
Finally write out your daily manifestation for what you choose to bring into your life, with gratitude and feeling
as if you already have it now (your manifestation may be the same as the day before but it's important to write it out).

AFFIRMATIONS	GRATITUDE	DAILY MANIFESTATION
# 1	# 1	
# 2	# 2	
# 3	# 3	

PLAN ~ ACTION ~ REWARD

PLAN   Write down the things you choose to ACHIEVE TODAY

ACTION   Write down THE TASKS to achieve your plan

REWARD   Write down how you will REWARD yourself for completing your plan

WRITE 1 POSITIVE BELIEF ABOUT YOURSELF BELOW:

QUOTE OF THE DAY

Life is about Fun and Happiness

PM

POSITIVITY

Write down something negative you experienced today - then under it list the positives you can take out of that experience

SELF LOVE

What activities have you done to nurture your love for yourself?

DOWNTIME / CHILL

What did you do to chill out today or to wind down and give yourself a break?

HOW HAPPY DID YOU FEEL TODAY?

 0   1   2   3   4   🙂   6   7   8   9   10   😄

USE ONE WORD TO DESCRIBE HOW YOU ARE FEELING:

WHAT DID YOU DO THAT WAS FUN TODAY?

ENERGY

WHAT'S BEEN DRAINING YOUR ENERGY TODAY?

WHAT'S BOOSTED YOUR ENERGY TODAY?

STRESS

WHAT'S ADDED TO THE STRESS IN YOUR DAY?

WHAT'S HELPED TO REDUCE YOUR STRESS TODAY?

AM

DATE:

Fill in 3 daily affirmations to keep your energy positive and build yourself up & 3 things you are grateful for.
Finally write out your daily manifestation for what you choose to bring into your life, with gratitude and feeling
as if you already have it now (your manifestation may be the same as the day before but it's important to write it out).

AFFIRMATIONS	GRATITUDE	DAILY MANIFESTATION
# 1	# 1	
# 2	# 2	
# 3	# 3	

PLAN ~ ACTION ~ REWARD

PLAN   Write down the things you choose to ACHIEVE TODAY

ACTION   Write down THE TASKS to achieve your plan

REWARD   Write down how you will REWARD yourself for completing your plan

WRITE 1 POSITIVE BELIEF ABOUT YOURSELF BELOW:

QUOTE OF THE DAY

Commit to yourself and you can do anything

74

POSITIVITY

Write down something negative you experienced today - then under it list the positives you can take out of that experience

SELF LOVE

What activities have you done to nurture your love for yourself?

DOWNTIME / CHILL

What did you do to chill out today or to wind down and give yourself a break?

HOW HAPPY DID YOU FEEL TODAY?

 0 1 2 3 4 😐 6 7 8 9 10 😄

USE ONE WORD TO DESCRIBE HOW YOU ARE FEELING:

WHAT DID YOU DO THAT WAS FUN TODAY?

ENERGY

WHAT'S BEEN DRAINING YOUR ENERGY TODAY?

WHAT'S BOOSTED YOUR ENERGY TODAY?

STRESS

WHAT'S ADDED TO THE STRESS IN YOUR DAY?

WHAT'S HELPED TO REDUCE YOUR STRESS TODAY?

AM

DATE:

Fill in 3 daily affirmations to keep your energy positive and build yourself up & 3 things you are grateful for.
Finally write out your daily manifestation for what you choose to bring into your life, with gratitude and feeling
as if you already have it now (your manifestation may be the same as the day before but it's important to write it out).

AFFIRMATIONS	GRATITUDE	DAILY MANIFESTATION
# 1	# 1	
# 2	# 2	
# 3	# 3	

PLAN ~ ACTION ~ REWARD

PLAN Write down the things you choose to ACHIEVE TODAY

ACTION Write down THE TASKS to achieve your plan

REWARD Write down how you will REWARD yourself for completing your plan

WRITE 1 POSITIVE BELIEF ABOUT YOURSELF BELOW:

QUOTE OF THE DAY

Exercise your mind & soul as well as your body

POSITIVITY

Write down something negative you experienced today - then under it list the positives you can take out of that experience

SELF LOVE

What activities have you done to nurture your love for yourself?

DOWNTIME / CHILL

What did you do to chill out today or to wind down and give yourself a break?

HOW HAPPY DID YOU FEEL TODAY?

 0   1   2   3   4   6   7   8   9   10   😄

USE ONE WORD TO DESCRIBE HOW YOU ARE FEELING:

WHAT DID YOU DO THAT WAS FUN TODAY?

ENERGY

WHAT'S BEEN DRAINING YOUR ENERGY TODAY?

WHAT'S BOOSTED YOUR ENERGY TODAY?

STRESS

WHAT'S ADDED TO THE STRESS IN YOUR DAY?

WHAT'S HELPED TO REDUCE YOUR STRESS TODAY?

DAY 29

 AM

DATE:

Fill in 3 daily affirmations to keep your energy positive and build yourself up & 3 things you are grateful for.
Finally write out your daily manifestation for what you choose to bring into your life, with gratitude and feeling
as if you already have it now (your manifestation may be the same as the day before but it's important to write it out).

AFFIRMATIONS	GRATITUDE	DAILY MANIFESTATION
# 1	# 1	
# 2	# 2	
# 3	# 3	

PLAN ~ ACTION ~ REWARD

PLAN   Write down the things you choose to ACHIEVE TODAY

ACTION   Write down THE TASKS to achieve your plan

REWARD   Write down how you will REWARD yourself for completing your plan

👍👎 👍👎 👍👎 👍👎 👍👎 👍👎

WRITE 1 POSITIVE BELIEF ABOUT YOURSELF BELOW:

QUOTE OF THE DAY

Consciously Connect to create a positive life

POSITIVITY

Write down something negative you experienced today - then under it list the positives you can take out of that experience

SELF LOVE

What activities have you done to nurture your love for yourself?

DOWNTIME / CHILL

What did you do to chill out today or to wind down and give yourself a break?

HOW HAPPY DID YOU FEEL TODAY?

 0 1 2 3 4 🙄 6 7 8 9 10 😄

USE ONE WORD TO DESCRIBE HOW YOU ARE FEELING:

WHAT DID YOU DO THAT WAS FUN TODAY?

ENERGY

WHAT'S BEEN DRAINING YOUR ENERGY TODAY?

WHAT'S BOOSTED YOUR ENERGY TODAY?

STRESS

WHAT'S ADDED TO THE STRESS IN YOUR DAY?

WHAT'S HELPED TO REDUCE YOUR STRESS TODAY?

DATE:

Fill in 3 daily affirmations to keep your energy positive and build yourself up & 3 things you are grateful for.
Finally write out your daily manifestation for what you choose to bring into your life, with gratitude and feeling
as if you already have it now (your manifestation may be the same as the day before but it's important to write it out).

AFFIRMATIONS	GRATITUDE	DAILY MANIFESTATION
# 1	# 1	
# 2	# 2	
# 3	# 3	

PLAN ~ ACTION ~ REWARD

PLAN — Write down the things you choose to ACHIEVE TODAY

ACTION — Write down THE TASKS to achieve your plan

REWARD — Write down how you will REWARD yourself for completing your plan

WRITE 1 POSITIVE BELIEF ABOUT YOURSELF BELOW:

QUOTE OF THE DAY

Commit to change, find your Courage & create a Confident you

POSITIVITY

Write down something negative you experienced today - then under it list the positives you can take out of that experience

SELF LOVE

What activities have you done to nurture your love for yourself?

DOWNTIME / CHILL

What did you do to chill out today or to wind down and give yourself a break?

HOW HAPPY DID YOU FEEL TODAY?

 0   1   2   3   4   6   7   8   9   10   😄

USE ONE WORD TO DESCRIBE HOW YOU ARE FEELING:

WHAT DID YOU DO THAT WAS FUN TODAY?

ENERGY

WHAT'S BEEN DRAINING YOUR ENERGY TODAY?

WHAT'S BOOSTED YOUR ENERGY TODAY?

STRESS

WHAT'S ADDED TO THE STRESS IN YOUR DAY?

WHAT'S HELPED TO REDUCE YOUR STRESS TODAY?

FINAL 30 DAY CHECK-IN
YOU MADE IT, WAY TO GO!

This is where you can reflect on what you have learnt about yourself.
What are the key takeaways from your 30 day journey?

How do you feel you have changed?
(what have you let go of, what are you doing differently, what are you now aware of?)

What are you still struggling with, what is getting in the way that you still want to shift?

What are you planning to do in order to break through these struggles?

Don't stop now, keep going!
Life is all about your journey, where we are continually working on improving and shifting the barriers in our way. What are your intentions to continue lifting into your power over the next 30 days?

CONGRATULATIONS
YOU MADE IT, WAY TO GO!

Congratulations on completing your 30 day Wellness Mindset journey. I hope you have enjoyed your experience and have got to know yourself better. By completing the month you have shifted and lifted your energy to step further into your confidence and self awareness.

As you become more consciously connected and aware of yourself and your routine actions - the lights turn on as you begin to understand yourself more fully. You start to feel lighter and more peaceful and calm as you let go of the things that are weighing you down. When you let shit go - and focus on what's really important you can shift n lift yourself into a happier place with less stress and more energy. You can simplify your life!

YOUR PERSONAL DECODING SESSION
QUICK & EASY EXCERCISE

Just straight off the top of your head,
pick a number between 1 and 9.

1 2 3 4 5 6 7 8 9

TURN THE PAGE **ONLY** ONCE
YOU HAVE SELECTED YOUR NUMBER

YOUR PERSONAL DECODING SESSION
UNDERSTANDING YOUR NUMBER

This simple decoding exercise allows you to tap into your unconscious mind and receive a message from your higher self. The message you have received is to help you have greater awareness of which area in your life needs more focus for you at this point in time. It will be the greatest area in your life where you can create positive change.

Which area of your life will allow you to create the greatest positive change?

1 Your Self and Your Health
2 Your Partner - in work or your relationship
3 Your Family - immediate or extended
4 Your Friends
5 Your Work and Career
6 Your Purpose in life
7 Your Finances
8 Your Lifestyle
9 Your Journey in Life

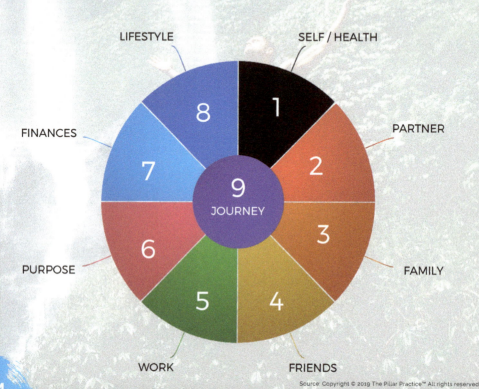

NAME _____ DATE _____ / _____ / _____

WHERE YOU ARE 30 DAYS LATER SNAPSHOT - SELF ASSESSMENT

Now you have completed your 30 Day Mindfulness Journey, complete your 30 day self assessment below by circling honestly where you are now in each of the fields. This will help you measure how far you have come.

AFFIRMATIONS	NEVER	SOMETIMES	WEEKLY	DAILY				
MANIFESTING	NEVER	SOMETIMES	WEEKLY	DAILY				
GRATITUDE	NEVER	SOMETIMES	WEEKLY	DAILY				
MEDITATION	NEVER	SOMETIMES	WEEKLY	DAILY				
EXERCISE	NEVER	SOMETIMES	1X WEEK	2X WEEK	3X WEEK +			
NUTRITION	UNHEALTHY	0	1	2	3	4	5	HEALTHY/BALANCED
WATER INTAKE	NONE	0	1	2	3	4	5	2+ LITRES A DAY
SLEEP QUALITY	NOT RESTED	0	1	2	3	4	5	WELL RESTED
ME TIME	NONE AT ALL	0	1	2	3	4	5	EVERYDAY
SELF LOVE	LOW	0	1	2	3	4	5	HIGH
SELF TALK/HEAD TALK	NEGATIVE	0	1	2	3	4	5	POSITIVE
OVERALL FEELING	STUCK/DOWN	0	1	2	3	4	5	HAPPY/BALANCED
OVERALL HAPPINESS	NOT HAPPY	0	1	2	3	4	5	VERY HAPPY
OVERALL STRESS	LOW STRESS	0	1	2	3	4	5	HIGH STRESS
OVERALL ENERGY	LOW ENERGY	0	1	2	3	4	5	HIGH ENERGY
OVERALL FUN	NO FUN	0	1	2	3	4	5	LOADS OF FUN

WANT TO CONTINUE YOUR WELLNESS JOURNEY?

FIND OUT BY
BOOKING IN YOUR **FREE
PATH TO CHANGE SESSION**

· · · · · · · · · · · · · · · · · · ·

HTTPS://CALENDLY.COM/
SALLY-ESTLIN/PATH-TO-CHANGE

Dedicated to :

~ Jackson, Charli, Tommy, Sam & my inner circle of friends ~
I'm so very grateful for you opening my eyes to what's really important in life and
providing the opportunity for me to become consciously connected to my abundant life.

CONSCIOUSLY CONNECT

Start with simple, small steps
This is where you shift the obstacles
& lift into your greatness!

Sally

www.holisticallyfit.com.au

Book Design & Collaboration by Teresa Armytage / Wellnesspreneur
www.wellnesspreneur.com.au

All content pertaining to Coding, Decoding and Recoding: Copyright © 2019 The Pillar Practice™ All rights reserved

First Printing 2019

ISBN 978-0-6468-0387-6

Ingram Spark Publishing

www.ingramspark.com

Ingram Content Group
1 Ingram Blvd.
LaVergne, TN. 37086n:

Printed on demand

Front cover photograph copyright © 2019 by Dudarev Mikhail/ Climbing girl 690366619/Shutterstock Images

Back cover photograph copyright © 2019 by Puhhha/ waterfall 437334607/Shutterstock Images

ARTWORK/PHOTOGRAPHY CREDITS

BACK COVER IMAGE
PHOTO BY PUHHHA
WATERFALL 437334607
SHUTTERSTOCK IMAGES

WOODEN BRIDGE
PHOTO BY KAIQUE ROCHA
ON PEXELS.COM

NORTHERN LIGHTS
PHOTO BY NAIAN WANG
ON UNSPLASH.COM

FRONT COVER IMAGE
PHOTO BY DUDAREV MIKHAI
CLIMBING GIRL 690366619
SHUTTERSTOCK IMAGES

ORANGE STAIRS
PHOTO BY AMBROSE
CHUA ON UNSPLASH

GREEN WATER REFLECTION
PHOTO BY PIXABAY
ON PEXELS.COM

HAND HOLDING LENS
PHOTO BY PAUL SKORUPSKAS
ON UNSPLASH.COM

MAN RAISING HANDS
PHOTO BY SNAPWIRE
ON PEXELS.COM

CHESS PIECES
PHOTO BY SEBASTIAN VOORTMAN
ON PEXELS.COM

SMILEY FACE ICONS
DESIGNED BY FREEPIC

RISING MOON
PHOTO BY ALEX ANDREWS
ON PEXELS.COM

SUNSET SILHOUETTE
PHOYO BY NA INHO
ON UNSPLASH.COM

Printed in Australia
AUHW012352270322
361452AU00005B/10

9 780646 803876